A Woman's Book of God's Promises

A Woman's Book of God's Promises

Copyright © 1996 by Garborg's Heart 'n Home, Inc.

All text in this book has been taken from *The Message* © by Eugene H. Peterson, 1996. All rights reserved. Published by permission of NavPress, P.O. Box 35001, Colorado Springs, CO 80933, and in association with the literary agency of Alive Communications, Inc., 1465 Kelly Johnson Blvd., Suite 320, Colorado Springs, CO 80920.

The Message is a contemporary rendering of the Bible from the original languages, crafted to present its tone, rhythm, events, and ideas in everyday speech.

Published by Garborg's Heart 'n Home, Inc., P.O. Box 20132, Bloomington, MN 55420

Art: Eric Lessing/Art Resource, NY

Monet, Claude. *Les Coqueliquote* (or *The Poppy Field*), 1873. Musee d'Orsay, Paris, France.

All rights reserved. No part of this book may be reproduced in any form without permission in writing from the publisher.

SPCN 5-5044-0299-9

Now we look inside, and what we see is that anyone united with the Messiah gets a fresh start, is created new. The old life is gone; a new life burgeons! Look at it! All this comes from the God who settled the relationship between us and him, and then called us to settle our relationships with each other.

2 Corinthians 5:17-18

May God, who puts all things together, makes all things whole...
Who led Jesus, our Great Shepherd,
up and alive from the dead,
Now put you together, provide you
with everything you need to please him...
by means of the sacrifice of Jesus, the Messiah.
All glory to Jesus forever and always!

Hebrews 13:20-21

December 31

*N*ot for our sake, GOD, no, not for our sake,
but for your name's sake, show your glory.
Do it on account of your merciful love,
do it on account of your faithful ways.

Psalm 115:1

Be good to your servant, GOD; be as good as your Word. Train me in good common sense; I'm thoroughly committed to living your way. Before I learned to answer you, I wandered all over the place, but now I'm in step with your Word. You are good, and the source of good; train me in your goodness.

Psalm 119:65-68

December 30

𝓛ong, long ago [God] decided to adopt us into his family through Jesus Christ. (What pleasure he took in planning this!) He wanted us to enter into the celebration of his lavish gift-giving by the hand of his beloved Son.

Ephesians 1:5-6

What's the price of two or three pet canaries? Some loose change, right? But God never overlooks a single one. And he pays even greater attention to you, down to the last detail—even numbering the hairs on your head! So don't be intimidated.... You're worth more than a million canaries.

Luke 12:6-7

December 29

 truly delight in God's commands, but it's pretty obvious that not all of me joins in that delight. Parts of me covertly rebel, and just when I least expect it, they take charge. I've tried everything and nothing helps. I'm at the end of my rope. Is there no one who can do anything for me? Isn't that the real question? The answer, thank God, is that Jesus Christ can and does.

Romans 7:22-25

There's nothing like the written Word of God for showing you the way to salvation through faith in Christ Jesus. Every part of Scripture is God-breathed and useful one way or another—showing us truth, exposing our rebellion, correcting our mistakes, training us to live God's way. Through the Word we are put together and shaped up for the tasks God has for us.

2 Timothy 3:15-17

December 28

This is my command: Love one another the way I loved you. This is the very best way to love. Put your life on the line for your friends. You are my friends when you do the things I command you. I'm no longer calling you servants because servants don't understand what their master is thinking and planning. No, I've named you friends because I've let you in on everything I've heard from the Father.

John 15:12-15

January 5

Since this is the kind of life we have chosen, the life of the Spirit...we will not compare ourselves with each other as if one of us were better and another worse. We have far more interesting things to do with our lives. Each of us is an original.

Galatians 5:25-26

December 27

I'm asking GOD for one thing, only one thing:
To live with him in his house my whole life long. I'll
contemplate his beauty; I'll study at his feet. That's
the only quiet, secure place in a noisy world.

Psalm 27:4-5

January 6

Then the star appeared again, the same star they had seen in the eastern skies. It led them on until it hovered over the place of the child. They could hardly contain themselves: They were in the right place! They had arrived at the right time! They entered the house and saw the child in the arms of Mary, his mother. Overcome, they kneeled and worshiped him. Then they...presented gifts: gold, frankincense, myrrh.

Matthew 2:9-11

December 26

There is a nice symmetry in this: Death initially came by a man, and resurrection from death came by a man. Everybody dies in Adam; everybody comes alive in Christ. But we have to wait our turn: Christ is first, then those with him at his Coming, the grand consummation when, after crushing the opposition, he hands over his kingdom to God the Father.

1 Corinthians 15:21-24

At once the angel was joined by a
huge angelic choir singing God's praises:
"Glory to God in the heavenly heights,
Peace to all men and women on earth who please him."

Luke 2:13-14

Open your mouth and taste, open your eyes and see—
how good GOD is.
Blessed are you who run to him.
Worship GOD if you want the best;
worship opens doors to all his goodness.

Psalm 34:8-9

There were sheepherders camping in the neighborhood.... Suddenly, God's angel stood among them and God's glory blazed around them. They were terrified. The angel said, "Don't be afraid. I'm here to announce a great and joyful event that is meant for everybody, worldwide: A Savior has just been born in David's town, a Savior who is Messiah and Master."

Luke 2:8-11

December 24

God said, "Light up the darkness!" and our lives filled up with light as we saw and understood God in the face of Christ, all bright and beautiful. If you only look at us, you might well miss the brightness. We carry this precious Message around in the unadorned clay pots of our ordinary lives. That's to prevent anyone from confusing God's incomparable power with us.

2 Corinthians 4:5-7

January 9

So Joseph went from the Galilean town of Nazareth up to Bethlehem in Judah, David's town, for the census. As a descendant of David, he had to go there. He went with Mary, his fiancee, who was pregnant. While they were there, the time came for her to give birth. She gave birth to a son, her firstborn. She wrapped him in a blanket and laid him in a manger, because there was no room in the hostel.

Luke 2:4-7

December 23

When two of you get together on anything at all on earth and make a prayer of it, my Father in heaven goes into action. And when two or three of you are together because of me, you can be sure that I'll be there.

Matthew 18:19-20

Mary was engaged to be married to Joseph. Before they came to the marriage bed, Joseph discovered she was pregnant.... God's angel spoke in [a] dream: "Joseph, son of David, don't hesitate to get married. Mary's pregnancy is Spirit-conceived.... She will bring a son to birth, and when she does, you, Joseph, will name him Jesus—'God saves'— because he will save his people from their sins."

Matthew 1:18-21

December 22

The fulfillment of God's promise depends entirely on trusting God and his way, and then simply embracing him and what he does. God's promise arrives as pure gift. That's the only way everyone can be sure to get in on it, those who keep the religious traditions *and* those who have never heard of them.

Romans 4:16

And Mary said, "I'm bursting with God-news; I'm dancing the song of my Savior God. God took one good look at me, and look what happened—I'm the most fortunate woman on earth! What God has done for me will never be forgotten, the God whose very name is holy, set apart from all others."

Luke 1:46-48

Be content with who you are, and don't put on airs. God's strong hand is on you; he'll promote you at the right time. Live carefree before God; he is most careful with you.

1 Peter 5:6-7

The angel assured her, "Mary, you have nothing to fear. God has a surprise for you: You will become pregnant and give birth to a son and call his name Jesus. He will be great, be called 'Son of the Highest.' The Lord God will give him the throne of his father David; He will rule Jacob's house forever—no end, ever, to his kingdom."

Luke 1:30-33

He heals the heartbroken
and bandages their wounds.
He counts the stars
and assigns each a name.
Our Lord is great, with limitless strength;
we'll never comprehend what he knows and does.

Psalm 147:3-5

January 13

God sent the angel Gabriel to the Galilean village of Nazareth to a virgin engaged to be married to a man descended from David. His name was Joseph, and the virgin's name, Mary. Upon entering, Gabriel greeted her: "Good morning! You're beautiful with God's beauty, Beautiful inside and out! God be with you."

Luke 1:26-28

December 19

But now that you've found you don't have to listen to sin tell you what to do, and have discovered the delight of listening to God telling you, what a surprise! A whole, healed, put-together life right now, with more and more of life on the way! Work hard for sin your whole life and your pension is death. But God's gift is real life, eternal life, delivered by Jesus, our Master.

Romans 6:22-23

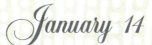

We all live off his generous bounty,
gift after gift after gift....
this exuberant giving and receiving,
This endless knowing and understanding—
all this came through Jesus, the Messiah.

John 1:16-17

All the things I once thought were so important are gone from my life. Compared to the high privilege of knowing Christ Jesus as my Master, firsthand, everything I once thought I had going for me is insignificant.... I've dumped it all in the trash so that I could embrace Christ and be embraced by him.

Philippians 3:8-9

The Word became flesh and blood,
and moved into the neighborhood.
We saw the glory with our own eyes,
the one-of-a-kind glory,
like Father, like Son,
Generous inside and out,
true from start to finish.

John 1:14

December 17

𝒥 ask him that with both feet planted firmly on love, you'll be able to take in with all Christians the extravagant dimensions of Christ's love. Reach out and experience the breadth! Test its length! Plumb the depths! Rise to the heights! Live full lives, full in the fullness of God.

Ephesians 3:17-18

He came to his own people, but they didn't want him. But whoever did want him, who believed he was who he claimed and would do what he said, he made to be their true selves, their child-of-God selves. These are the God-begotten.

John 1:11-13

December 16

$\mathcal{E}$mbrace this God-life. Really embrace it, and nothing will be too much for you.... That's why I urge you to pray for absolutely everything, ranging from small to large. Include everything as you embrace this God-life, and you'll get God's everything.

Mark 11:22-24

Everything was created through him;
nothing—not one thing!—
came into being without him.
What came into existence was Life,
and the Life was Light to live by.
The Life-Light blazed out of the darkness;
the darkness couldn't put it out.

John 1:3-5

December 15

Search high and low, scan skies and land,
you'll find nothing and no one quite like GOD.
The holy angels are in awe before him;
he looms immense and august over everyone around him.
GOD…who is like you,
powerful and faithful from every angle?

Psalm 89:6-8

January 18

The Word was first,
the Word present to God,
God present to the Word.
The Word was God,
in readiness for God from day one.

John 1:1-2

December 14

Worship the Lord your God and only the Lord your God. Serve him with absolute single-heartedness.

Luke 4:8

January 19

This is how much God loved the world: He gave his Son, his one and only Son. And this is why: so that no one need be destroyed; by believing in him, anyone can have a whole and lasting life. God didn't go to all the trouble of sending his Son merely to point an accusing finger, telling the world how bad it was. He came to help, to put the world right again.

John 3:16-17

Now that we know what we have—Jesus, this great High Priest with ready access to God—let's not let it slip through our fingers. We don't have a priest who is out of touch with our reality. He's been through weakness and testing, experienced it all—all but the sin. So let's walk right up to him and get what he is so ready to give. Take the mercy, accept the help.

Hebrews 4:14-16

January 20

"Don't push these children away. Don't ever get between them and me. These children are at the very center of life in the kingdom. Mark this: Unless you accept God's kingdom in the simplicity of a child, you'll never get in." Then, gathering the children up in his arms, he laid his hands of blessing on them.

Mark 10:14-16

December 12

"Teacher, which command in God's Law is the most important?" Jesus said, "'Love the Lord your God with all your passion and prayer and intelligence.' This is the most important, the first on any list. But there is a second to set alongside it: 'Love others as well as you love yourself.' These two commands are pegs; everything in God's Law and the Prophets hangs from them."

Matthew 22:36-40

January 21

So, what do you think? With God on our side like this, how can we lose? If God didn't hesitate to put everything on the line for us, embracing our condition and exposing himself to the worst by sending his own Son, is there anything else he wouldn't gladly and freely do for us?

Romans 8:31-32

December 11

It's who you are and the way you live that count before God. Your worship must engage your spirit in the pursuit of truth. That's the kind of people the Father is out looking for: those who are simply and honestly themselves before him in their worship. God is sheer being itself—Spirit. Those who worship him must do it out of their very being, their spirits, their true selves, in adoration.

John 4:23-24

January 22

But when the time arrived that was set by God the Father, God sent his Son, born among us of a woman, born under the conditions of the law so that he might redeem those of us who have been kidnapped by the law. Thus we have been set free to experience our rightful heritage.

Galatians 4:4-5

God's various gifts are handed out everywhere; but they all originate in God's Spirit. God's various ministries are carried out everywhere; but they all originate in God's Spirit. God's various expressions of power are in action everywhere; but God himself is behind it all. Each person is given something to do that shows who God is: Everyone gets in on it, everyone benefits.

1 Corinthians 12:4-7

January 23

What happens when we live God's way? He brings gifts into our lives, much the same way that fruit appears in an orchard—things like affection for others, exuberance about life, serenity. We develop a willingness to stick with things, a sense of compassion in the heart, and a conviction that a basic holiness permeates things and people.

Galatians 5:22-23

December 9

*L*ook at...our faces, shining with
your gracious anointing.
All sunshine and sovereign is GOD,
generous in gifts and glory.

Psalm 84:9,11

January 24

You are familiar with the generosity of our Master,
Jesus Christ. Rich as he was, he gave it all away for us—
in one stroke he became poor and we became rich.

2 Corinthians 8:9

December 8

Friends, when life gets really difficult, don't jump to the conclusion that God isn't on the job. Instead, be glad that you are in the very thick of what Christ experienced. This is a spiritual refining process, with glory just around the corner.

1 Peter 4:12-13

*L*et me give you a new command: Love one another.
In the same way I loved you, you love one another. This is
how everyone will recognize that you are my disciples—
when they see the love you have for each other.

John 13:34-35

December 7

Living then, as every one of you does, in pure grace, it's important that you not misinterpret yourselves as people who are bringing this goodness to God. No, God brings it all to you. The only accurate way to understand ourselves is by what God is and by what he does for us, not by what we are and what we do for him.

Romans 12:3

January 26

I didn't want some petty, inferior brand of righteousness that comes from keeping a list of rules when I could get the robust kind that comes from trusting Christ— God's righteousness. I gave up all that inferior stuff so I could know Christ personally, experience his resurrection power…. If there was any way to get in on the resurrection from the dead, I wanted to do it.

Philippians 3:9-11

December 6

No doubt about it! God is good—
good to good people, good to the good-hearted.
But I nearly missed it, missed seeing his goodness.
I was looking the other way....
I'm still in your presence, but you've taken my hand.
You wisely and tenderly lead me,
and then you bless me.

Psalm 73:1-3,23-24

January 27

Through the heartfelt mercies of our God,
God's Sunrise will break in upon us,
Shining on those in the darkness,
those sitting in the shadow of death,
Then showing us the way, one foot at a time,
down the path of peace.

Luke 1:78-79

December 5

The basic reality of God is plain enough. Open your eyes and there it is! By taking a long and thoughtful look at what God has created, people have always been able to see what their eyes as such can't see: eternal power, for instance, and the mystery of his divine being. So nobody has a good excuse.

Romans 1:19-20

We know very well that we are not set right with God by rule keeping but only through personal faith in Jesus Christ. How do we know? We tried it—and we had the best system of rules the world has ever seen! Convinced that no human being can please God by self-improvement, we believed in Jesus as the Messiah so that we might be set right before God by trusting in the Messiah, not by trying to be good.

Galatians 2:16

*L*ive in me. Make your home in me just as I do in you. In the same way that a branch can't bear grapes by itself but only by being joined to the vine, you can't bear fruit unless you are joined with me.

John 15:4

January 29

Trust GOD from the bottom of your heart;
don't try to figure out everything on your own.
Listen for GOD's voice in everything you do,
everywhere you go;
he's the one who will keep you on track.

Proverbs 3:5-6

December 3

How blessed is God! And what a blessing he is!
He's the Father of our Master, Jesus Christ, and takes
us to the high places of blessing in him. Long before
he laid down earth's foundations, he had us in mind,
had settled on us as the focus of his love, to be
made whole and holy by his love.

Ephesians 1:3-4

January 30

$\mathscr{I}$ am the Good Shepherd. The Good Shepherd puts the sheep before himself, sacrifices himself if necessary.... I know my own sheep and my own sheep know me.

John 10:11,14

December 2

The right word at the right time
is like a custom-made piece of jewelry,
And a wise friend's timely reprimand
is like a gold ring slipped on your finger.

Proverbs 25:11-12

January 31

Think of yourselves the way Christ Jesus thought of himself. He had equal status with God but didn't think so much of himself that he had to cling to the advantages of that status no matter what. Not at all. When the time came, he set aside the privileges of deity and took on the status of a slave, became *human*!

Philippians 2:5-7

....

December 1

*You're my place of quiet retreat;
I wait for your Word to renew me...
therefore I lovingly embrace everything you say.*

Psalm 119:114,119

You can tell for sure that you are now fully adopted as his own children because God sent the Spirit of his Son into our lives crying out, "Papa! Father!" Doesn't that privilege of intimate conversation with God make it plain that you are not a slave, but a child? And if you are a child, you're also an heir, with complete access to the inheritance.

Galatians 4:6-7

November 30

*I saw God before me for all time.
Nothing can shake me; he's right by my side.
I'm glad from the inside out, ecstatic;
I've pitched my tent in the land of hope....
You've got my feet on the life-path,
with your face shining sun-joy all around.*

Acts 2:25-28

If you don't know what you're doing, pray to the Father. He loves to help. You'll get his help, and won't be condescended to when you ask for it. Ask boldly, believingly, without a second thought.

James 1:5-6

November 29

Open up before GOD, keep nothing back;
he'll do whatever needs to be done:
He'll validate your life in the clear light of day
and stamp you with approval at high noon.
Quiet down before GOD,
be prayerful before him.

Psalm 37:5-7

ℒet's not allow ourselves to get fatigued doing good. At the right time we will harvest a good crop if we don't give up, or quit. Right now, therefore, every time we get the chance, let us work for the benefit of all, starting with the people closest to us in the community of faith.

Galatians 6:9,10

November 28

Your body has many parts—limbs, organs, cells—but no matter how many parts you can name, you're still one body.... The way God designed our bodies is a model for understanding our lives together as a church: every part dependent on every other part.... You are Christ's body—that's who you are! You must never forget this. Only as you accept your part of that body does your "part" mean anything.

1 Corinthians 12:12, 25-28

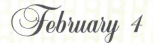

February 4

You, who made me stare trouble in the face,
Turn me around;
Now let me look life in the face. I've been to the bottom;
Bring me up, streaming with honors;
turn to me, be tender to me,
And I'll take up the lute and thank you
to the tune of your faithfulness, God.

Psalm 71:20-22

November 27

Hallelujah! Praise GOD from heaven,
praise him from the mountaintops;
Praise him, all you his angels...
praise him, you morning stars;
Praise him, high heaven,
praise him, heavenly rain clouds;
Praise, oh let them praise the name of GOD—
he spoke the word, and there they were!

Psalm 148:1-5

February 5

*I've already run for dear life straight to the arms of GOD.
So why would I run away now when you say,
"Run to the mountains..."?
GOD hasn't moved to the mountains;
his holy address hasn't changed.
He's in charge, as always.*

Psalm 11:1,4

Through him we received both the generous gift of his life and the urgent task of passing it on to others who receive it by entering into obedient trust in Jesus. You are who you are through this gift and call of Jesus Christ!

Romans 1:5-6

February 6

*L*et the peace of Christ keep you in tune with each other, in step with each other. None of this going off and doing your own thing. And cultivate thankfulness. Let the Word of Christ—the Message—have the run of the house. Give it plenty of room in your lives....
And sing, sing your hearts out to God!

Colossians 3:15-16

Rescue the perishing;
don't hesitate to step in and help.
If you say, "Hey, that's none of my business,"
will that get you off the hook?
Someone is watching you closely, you know—
Someone not impressed with weak excuses.

Proverbs 24:11-12

February 7

*Show me how you work, G*OD;
School me in your ways.
Take me by the hand;
Lead me down the path of truth...
Mark the milestones of your mercy and love, G*OD*.

Psalm 25:4-6

November 24

God is a safe place to hide, ready to help when we need him. We stand fearless at the cliff-edge of doom,
courageous in seastorm and earthquake,
Before the rush and roar of oceans,
the tremors that shift mountains....
God fights for us.

Psalm 46:1-3

February 8

Just think—you don't need a thing, you've got it all! All God's gifts are right in front of you.... And not only that, but God himself is right alongside to keep you steady and on track until things are all wrapped up by Jesus. God, who got you started in this spiritual adventure, shares with us the life of his Son and our Master Jesus. He will never give up on you. Never forget that.

1 Corinthians 1:7-9

November 23

$\mathcal{N}$ow I'm turning you over to God, our marvelous God whose gracious Word can make you into what he wants you to be and give you everything you could possibly need.... I have demonstrated to you how necessary it is to work on behalf of the weak and not exploit them. You'll not likely go wrong here if you keep remembering that our Master said, "You're far happier giving than getting."

Acts 20:32-35

February 9

*Isn't everything you *have* and everything you *are*
sheer gifts from God?... You already have all you need.*

1 Corinthians 4:7-8

November 22

God does not respond to what *we* do; we respond to what *God* does. We've finally figured it out. Our lives get in step with God and all others by letting him set the pace, not by proudly or anxiously trying to run the parade.

Romans 3:27-28

Everything God created is good, and to be received with thanks.... God's Word and our prayers make every item in creation holy.

1 Timothy 4:4-5

November 21

Your thoughts—how rare, how beautiful!
God, I'll never comprehend them!
I couldn't even begin to count them—
any more than I could count the sand of the sea.
Oh, let me rise in the morning and live always with you!

Psalm 139:17-18

*Our Lord is great, with limitless strength;
we'll never comprehend what he knows and does....
Sing to GOD a thanksgiving hymn,
play music on your instruments to God.*

Psalm 147:5,7

So spacious is [Christ], so roomy, that everything of God finds its proper place in him without crowding. Not only that, but all the broken and dislocated pieces of the universe— people and things, animals and atoms—get properly fixed and fit together in vibrant harmonies, all because of his death, his blood that poured down from the Cross.

Colossians 1:19-20

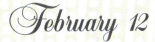

The blessing and glory and wisdom and thanksgiving,
The honor and power and strength,
To our God forever and ever and ever!

Revelation 7:12

November 19

Pure gold put in the fire comes out of it proved pure; genuine faith put through this suffering comes out proved genuine. When Jesus wraps this all up, it's your faith, not your gold, that God will have on display as evidence of his victory.

1 Peter 1:7

February 13

We respect our own parents for training and not spoiling us, so why not embrace God's training so we can truly *live*? While we were children, our parents did what *seemed* best to them. But God is doing what *is* best for us, training us to live God's holy best.

Hebrews 12:9-10

*L*ove...puts up with anything,
Trusts God always,
Always looks for the best,
Never looks back,
But keeps going to the end.
Love never dies.

1 Corinthians 13:4,7-8

February 14

What a beautiful thing, GOD, to give thanks,
to sing an anthem to you, the High God!
To announce your love each daybreak,
sing your faithful presence all through the night.

Psalm 92:1-2

November 17

Look at me. I stand at the door. I knock. If you hear me call and open the door, I'll come right in and sit down to supper with you. Conquerors will sit alongside me at the head table, just as I, having conquered, took the place of honor at the side of my Father. That's my gift to the conquerors!

Revelation 3:20-21

February 15

You trust God, don't you? Trust me. There is plenty of room for you in my Father's home. If that weren't so, would I have told you that I'm on my way to get a room ready for you? And if I'm on my way to get your room ready, I'll come back and get you so you can live where I live. And you already know the road I'm taking.

John 14:1-4

Every desirable and beneficial gift comes out of heaven. The gifts are rivers of light cascading down from the Father of Light.

James 1:17

February 16

*T*hank the miracle-working God,
His love never quits....
The God who laid out earth on ocean foundations,
His love never quits.
The God who filled the skies with light,
His love never quits.

Psalm 136:4,6-7

I look up to the mountains;
does my strength come from mountains?
No, my strength comes from GOD,
who made heaven, and earth, and mountains.
He won't let you stumble,
your Guardian God won't fall asleep.

Psalm 121:1-3

....

February 17

𝒥esus provided far more God-revealing signs than are written down in this book. These are written down so you will believe that Jesus is the Messiah, the Son of God, and in the of believing, have real and eternal life.... There are so many other things Jesus did. If they were all written down, each of them, one by one, I can't imagine a world big enough to hold such a library of books.

John 20:30-31; 21:25

That's what baptism into the life of Jesus means. When we are lowered into the water, it is like the burial of Jesus; when we are raised up out of the water, it is like the resurrection of Jesus. Each of us is raised into a light-filled world by our Father so that we can see where we're going in our new grace-sovereign country.

Romans 6:3

February 18

If each grain of sand on the seashore were numbered
and the sum labeled "chosen of God,"
They'd be numbers still, not names;
salvation comes by personal selection.
God doesn't count us; he calls us by name.

Romans 9:27

*G*OD is fair and just;
He corrects the misdirected,
Sends them in the right direction....
From now on every road you travel
Will take you to GOD.

Psalm 25:8-10

February 19

God is sheer mercy and grace; not easily angered, he's rich in love.... He doesn't treat us as our sins deserve, nor pay us back in full for our wrongs. As high as heaven is over the earth, so strong is his love to those who fear him. And as far as sunrise is from sunset, he has separated us from our sins.

Psalm 103:8,10-12

November 12

I have been crucified with Christ. My ego is no longer central. It is no longer important that I appear righteous before you or have your good opinion, and I am no longer driven to impress God. Christ lives in me. The life you see me living is not "mine," but it is lived by faith in the Son of God, who loved me and gave himself for me. I am not going to go back on that.

Galatians 2:20-21

February 20

It's in Christ that we find out who we are and what we are living for. Long before we first heard of Christ and got our hopes up, he had his eye on us, had designs on us for glorious living, part of the overall purpose he is working out in everything and everyone.

Ephesians 1:11

November 11

God will make you fit for what he's called you to be...he'll fill your good ideas and acts of faith with his own energy so that it all amounts to something. If your life honors the name of Jesus, he will honor you. Grace is behind and through all of this, our God giving himself freely, the Master, Jesus Christ, giving himself freely.

2 Thessalonians 1:11-12

Watch the way you talk.... Say only what helps, each word a gift.... Be gentle with one another, sensitive. Forgive one another as quickly and thoroughly as God in Christ forgave you.

Ephesians 4:29,32

*Generous in love—God, give grace!
Huge in mercy—wipe out my bad record....
Soak me in your laundry and I'll come out clean,
scrub me and I'll have a snow-white life.*

Psalm 51:1,7

February 22

No one's ever seen or heard anything like this,
Never so much as imagined anything quite like it—
What God has arranged for those who love him.

1 Corinthians 2:9

November 9

The ways of right-living people glow with light;
the longer they live, the brighter they shine....
Keep vigilant watch over your heart;
that's where life starts.

Proverbs 4:18,23

February 23

All this energy issues from Christ: God raised him from death and set him on a throne in deep heaven, in charge of running the universe, everything from galaxies to governments, no name and no power exempt from his rule. And not just for the time being, but *forever*. He is in charge of it all, has the final word on everything.

Ephesians 1:20-22

We who have run for our very lives to God have every reason to grab the promised hope with both hands and never let go. It's an unbreakable spiritual lifeline, reaching past all appearances right to the very presence of God where Jesus, running on ahead of us, has taken up his permanent post as high priest for us.

Hebrews 6:18-20

February 24

Anyone who sacrifices home, family, fields—whatever—because of me will get it all back a hundred times over, not to mention the considerable bonus of eternal life. This is the Great Reversal: many of the first ending up last, and the last first.

Matthew 19:29-30

Bless our God, oh peoples! Give him a thunderous welcome! Didn't he set us on the road to life?... He trained us first, passed us like silver through refining fires...pushed us to our very limit.... Finally he brought us to this well-watered place.

Psalm 66:8-12

February 25

Since God assured us, "I'll never let you down, never walk off and leave you," we can boldly quote,
"God is there, ready to help;
I'm fearless no matter what.
Who or what can get to me?"

Hebrews 13:5-6

....

November 6

Are you hurting? Pray. Do you feel great? Sing. Are you sick? Call the church leaders together to pray and anoint you with oil in the name of the Master. Believing-prayer will heal you, and Jesus will put you on your feet. And if you've sinned, you'll be forgiven—healed inside and out.

James 5:13-15

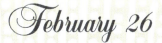

February 26

What a gift life is to those who stay the course!
You've heard, of course, of Job's staying power, and you
know how God brought it all together for him at the end.
That's because God cares, cares right down
to the last detail.

James 5:11

Take a good hard look at Jesus. He's the centerpiece
of everything we believe, faithful in everything
God gave him to do.

Hebrews 3:1-3

February 27

This is how God showed his love for us: God sent his only Son into the world so we might live through him. This is the kind of love we are talking about—not that we once upon a time loved God, but that he loved us and sent his Son as a sacrifice to clear away our sins and the damage they've done to our relationship with God.

1 John 4:9-10

November 4

Charm can mislead and beauty soon fades.
The woman to be admired and praised
is the woman who lives in the Fear-of-God.

Proverbs 31:30

February 28

Jesus said, "I am the Bread of Life.
The person who aligns with me hungers no more
and thirsts no more, ever.... Whoever believes
in me has real life, eternal life."

John 6:35,47

November 3

God's Spirit is right alongside helping us along. If we don't know how or what to pray, it doesn't matter. He does our praying in and for us, making prayer out of our wordless sighs, our aching groans. He knows us far better than we know ourselves...and keeps us present before God. That's why we can be so sure that every detail in our lives of love for God is worked into something good.

Romans 8:26-28

$\mathcal{L}$ive a lover's life, circumspect and exemplary, a life Jesus will be proud of: bountiful in fruits from the soul, making Jesus Christ attractive to all, getting everyone involved in the glory and praise of God.

Philippians 1:10-11

*M*y choice is you, GOD, first and only.
And now I find I'm *your* choice!...
You made me your heir!

Psalm 16:5-6

Trust steadily in God,
hope unswervingly,
love extravagantly.
And the best of the three is love.

1 Corinthians 13:13

November 1

All praise to the God and Father of our Master, Jesus the Messiah! Father of all mercy! God of all healing counsel! He comes alongside us when we go through hard times, and before you know it, he brings us alongside someone else who is going through hard times so that we can be there for that person just as God was there for us.

2 Corinthians 1:3-4

Ask and you'll get;
Seek and you'll find;
Knock and the door will open.
Don't bargain with God. Be direct.
Ask for what you need.

Luke 11:9-10

....

We're depending on GOD;
he's everything we need.
What's more, our hearts brim with joy
since we've taken for our own his holy name.
Love us, GOD, with all you've got—
that's what we're depending on.

Psalm 33:20-22

$\mathcal{T}$he world of the generous gets larger and larger...
The one who blesses others is abundantly blessed;
those who help others are helped.

Proverbs 11:24-25

*L*et's agree to use all our energy in getting along with each other. Help others with encouraging words; don't drag them down by finding fault.

Romans 14:19

Give your entire attention to what God is doing right now, and don't get worked up about what may or may not happen tomorrow. God will help you deal with whatever hard things come up when the time comes.

Matthew 6:34

October 29

$\mathcal{W}$here you are right now is God's place for you.
Live and obey and love and believe right there.

1 Corinthians 7:17

March 5

But you, dear friends, carefully build yourselves up in this most holy faith by praying in the Holy Spirit, staying right at the center of God's love, keeping your arms open and outstretched, ready for the mercy of our Master, Jesus Christ. This is the unending life, the *real* life!

Jude 1:20-21

For GOD is sheer beauty,
all-generous in love,
loyal always and ever.

Psalm 100:5

March 6

$\mathcal{L}$ive out your God-created identity. Live generously and graciously toward others, the way God lives toward you.

Matthew 5:48

𝒥esus…addressed them: "I am the world's Light. No one who follows me stumbles around in the darkness. I provide plenty of light to live in."

John 8:12

Hallelujah!
Praise God in his holy house of worship,
praise him under the open skies;
Praise him for his acts of power,
praise him for his magnificent greatness....
Let every living, breathing creature praise GOD!
Hallelujah!

Psalm 150:1-2,6

October 26

Go ahead and be angry. You do well to be angry—but don't use your anger as fuel for revenge. And don't stay angry. Don't go to bed angry. Don't give the Devil that kind of foothold in your life.

Ephesians 4:26-27

Starting from scratch, he made the entire human race and made the earth hospitable, with plenty of time and space for living so we could seek after God, and not just grope around in the dark but actually *find* him. He doesn't play hide-and-seek with us. He's not remote; he's *near*. We live and move in him, can't get away from him!

Acts 17:26-28

*Is there anyplace I can go to avoid your Spirit?
to be out of your sight?
If I climb to the sky, you're there!
If I go underground, you're there!
If I flew on morning's wings to the far western horizon,
You'd find me in a minute—you're already there waiting!*

Psalm 139:7-10

The fundamental fact of existence is that this trust in God, this faith, is the firm foundation under everything that makes life worth living. It's our handle on what we can't see.... By faith, we see the world called into existence by God's word, what we see created by what we don't see.

Hebrews 11:1,3

I write this, dear children, to guide you out of sin. But if anyone does sin, we have a Priest-Friend in the presence of the Father: Jesus Christ, righteous Jesus. When he served as a sacrifice for our sins, he solved the sin problem for good—not only ours, but the whole world's.

1 John 2:1-2

For God's Word is solid to the core;
everything he makes is sound inside and out....
Earth is drenched
in God's affectionate satisfaction.

Psalm 33:4-5

How exquisite your love, O God!
How eager we are to run under your wings,
To eat our fill at the banquet you spread
as you fill [us] with Eden spring water.
You're a fountain of cascading light,
and you open our eyes to light.

Psalm 36:7-9

March 11

If I give everything I own to the poor and even go to the stake to be burned as a martyr, but I don't love, I've gotten nowhere. So, no matter what I say, what I believe, and what I do, I'm bankrupt without love.

1 Corinthians 13:3

*A good woman is hard to find,
and worth far more than diamonds.
Her husband trusts her without reserve,
and never has reason to regret it.
Never spiteful, she treats him generously
all her life long.*

Proverbs 31:10-12

You're blessed when you're content with just who you are—no more, no less. That's the moment you find yourselves proud owners of everything that can't be bought. You're blessed when you've worked up a good appetite for God. He's food and drink in the best meal you'll ever eat.

Matthew 5:5-6

The spacious, free life is from GOD,
it's also protected and safe.
GOD-strengthened, we're delivered from evil—
when we run to him, he saves us.

Psalm 37:39-40

*G*o out and train everyone you meet, far and near, in this way of life, marking them by baptism in the threefold name: Father, Son, and Holy Spirit. Then instruct them in the practice of all I have commanded you. I'll be with you as you do this, day after day after day, right up to the end of the age.

Matthew 28:19-20

It's resurrection, resurrection, always resurrection, that undergirds what I do and say, the way I live.... It was sin that made death so frightening and law-code guilt that gave sin its leverage, its destructive power. But now in a single victorious stroke of Life, all three—sin, guilt, death—are gone, the gift of our Master, Jesus Christ. Thank God!

1 Corinthians 15:32,56-57

𝒥esus said, "I am the Road, also the Truth, also the Life. No one gets to the Father apart from me. If you really knew me, you would know my Father as well. From now on, you do know him. You've even seen him!"

John 14:6-7

October 19

He wants not only us but *everyone* saved, you know, everyone to get to know the truth *we've* learned: that there's one God and only one, and one Priest-Mediator between God and us—Jesus, who offered himself in exchange for everyone held captive by sin, to set them all free. Eventually the news is going to get out.

1 Timothy 2:4-6

*Oh, that my steps might be steady,
keeping to the course you set;
Then I'd never have any regrets
in comparing my life with your counsel.*

Psalm 119:5-6

....

October 18

Truth, righteousness, peace, faith, and salvation are more than words. Learn how to apply them. You'll need them throughout your life. God's Word is an indispensable weapon. In the same way, prayer is essential in this ongoing warfare. Pray hard and long.

Ephesians 6:14-18

𝓑y shifting our focus from what we do to what God does, don't we cancel out all our careful keeping of the rules and ways God commanded? Not at all. What happens, in fact, is that by putting that entire way of life in its proper place, we confirm it.

Romans 3:31

God, it seems you've been our home forever;
long before the mountains were born,
Long before you brought earth itself to birth,
from "once upon a time" to
"kingdom come"—you are God.

Psalm 90:1-2

My beloved friends, let us continue to love each other since love comes from God. Everyone who loves is born of God and experiences a relationship with God. The person who refuses to love doesn't know the first thing about God, because God *is* love—so you can't know him if you don't love.

1 John 4:7-8

October 16

We're not giving up. How could we! Even though on the outside it often looks like things are falling apart on us, on the inside, where God is making new life, not a day goes by without his unfolding grace.... There's far more here than meets the eye. The things we see now are here today, gone tomorrow. But the things we can't see now will last forever.

2 Corinthians 4:16,18

*G*OD is higher than anything and anyone,
outshining everything you can see in the skies.
Who can compare with GOD, our God,
so majestically enthroned,
Surveying his magnificent
heavens and earth?

Psalm 113:4-6

....

Be generous with me and I'll live a full life;
not for a minute will I take my eyes off your road.
Open my eyes so I can see
what you show me of your miracle-wonders.

Psalm 119:17-18

We know only a portion of the truth, and what we say about God is always incomplete. But when the Complete arrives, our incompletes will be canceled.... We don't yet see things clearly. We're squinting in a fog, peering through a mist. But it won't be long before the weather clears and the sun shines bright! We'll see it all then, see it all as clearly as God sees us, knowing him directly just as he knows us!

1 Corinthians 13:9-10

Just before the Passover Feast, Jesus knew that the time had come to leave this world to go to the Father. Having loved his dear companions, he continued to love them right to the end.

John 13:1

Walk into the fields and look at the wildflowers. They don't fuss with their appearance—but have you ever seen color and design quite like it? The ten best-dressed men and women in the country look shabby alongside them. If God gives such attention to the wildflowers, most of them never even seen, don't you think he'll attend to you, take pride in you, do his best for you?

Luke 12:27-28

Don't lose a minute in building on what you've been given, complementing your basic faith with good character, spiritual understanding, alert discipline, passionate patience, reverent wonder, warm friendliness, and generous love, each dimension fitting into and developing the others.

2 Peter 1:5

March 21

Gᴏᴅ's love, though, is ever and always,
eternally present to all who fear him,
Making everything right for them and their children
as they follow his Covenant ways
and remember to do whatever he said.
Gᴏᴅ has set his throne in heaven;
he rules over us all.

Psalm 103:17-19

Unless a grain of wheat is buried in the ground, dead to the world, it is never any more than a grain of wheat. But if it is buried, it sprouts and reproduces itself many times over. In the same way, anyone who holds on to life just as it is destroys that life. But if you let it go, reckless in your love, you'll have it forever, real and eternal.

John 12:24-25

The foundations of the City walls were garnished with every precious gem imaginable…the twelve gates were twelve pearls, each gate a single pearl. The main street of the City was pure gold, translucent as glass. But there was no sign of a Temple, for the Lord God—the Sovereign-Strong—and the Lamb are the Temple. The City doesn't need sun or moon for light. God's Glory is its light, the Lamb its lamp!

Revelation 21:19,21-23

The people gave him a wonderful welcome, some throwing their coats on the street, others spreading out rushes they had cut in the fields. Running ahead and following after, they were calling out,
"Hosanna!"
"Blessed is he who comes in God's name!"

Mark 11:8-9

If you're serious about living this new resurrection life with Christ, *act* like it. Pursue the things over which Christ presides. Don't shuffle along, eyes to the ground, absorbed with the things right in front of you. Look up, and be alert to what is going on around Christ—that's where the action is. See things from *his* perspective.

Colossians 3:1-2

$\mathcal{B}$e agreeable, be sympathetic, be loving, be compassionate, be humble...bless. You'll be a blessing and also get a blessing.

1 Peter 3:8-9

My purpose in writing is simply this: that you who believe in God's Son will know beyond the shadow of a doubt that you have eternal life, the reality and not the illusion. And how bold and free we then become in his presence, freely asking according to his will, sure that he's listening. And if we're confident that he's listening, we know that what we've asked for is as good as ours.

1 John 5:13-15

Is anyone thirsty? Come!
All who will, come and drink,
Drink freely of the Water of Life!

Revelation 22:17

March 25

Surprise us with love at daybreak;
then we'll skip and dance all the day long....
Let your servants see what you're best at—
the ways you rule and bless your children.
And let the loveliness of our Lord, our God, rest on us,
confirming the work that we do.
Oh, yes. Affirm the work that we do!

Psalm 90:14,16-17

October 8

Father, it's time. Display the bright splendor of your Son so the Son in turn may show your bright splendor. You put him in charge of everything human so he might give real and eternal life to all in his charge. And this is the real and eternal life: that they know you, the one and only true God, and Jesus Christ, whom you sent.

John 17:1-3

March 26

Isn't it obvious that God-talk without God-acts is outrageous nonsense?... You can no more show me your works apart from your faith than I can show you my faith apart from my works. Faith and works, works and faith, fit together hand in glove.... Faith expresses itself in works.

James 2:17-18, 22

You are right and you *do* right, GOD;
your decisions are right on target.
You rightly instruct us in how to live
ever faithful to you....
Your righteousness is eternally right,
your revelation is the only truth.

Psalm 119:137-138,142

It stands to reason, doesn't it, that if the alive-and-present God who raised Jesus from the dead moves into your life, he'll do the same thing in you that he did in Jesus, bringing you alive to himself? When God lives and breathes in you (and he does, as surely as he did in Jesus), you are delivered from that dead life. With his Spirit living in you, your body will be as alive as Christ's!

Romans 8:11

Since we've compiled this long and sorry record as sinners...and proved that we are utterly incapable of living the glorious lives God wills for us, God did it for us. Out of sheer generosity he put us in right standing with himself. A pure gift. He got us out of the mess we're in and restored us to where he always wanted us to be. And he did it by means of Jesus Christ.

Romans 3:23-24

You've always been great toward me—what love!
You snatched me from the brink of disaster!...
You, O God, are both tender and kind,
not easily angered, immense in love,
and you never, never quit.

Psalm 86:13,15

October 5

They took Jesus away. Carrying his cross, Jesus went out to the place called Skull Hill (the name in Hebrew is Golgotha), where they crucified him, and with him two others, one on each side, Jesus in the middle. Pilate wrote a sign and had it placed on the cross. It read:
JESUS THE NAZARENE
THE KING OF THE JEWS.

John 19:16-19

March 29

A crescendo of voices in Heaven sang out,
"The kingdom of the world is now
the Kingdom of our God and his Messiah!
He will rule forever and ever!"

Revelation 11:15

Oh yes, you shaped me first inside, then out;
you formed me in my mother's womb.
I thank you, High God—you're breathtaking!
Body and soul, I am marvelously made!
I worship in adoration—what a creation!

Psalm 139:13-14

Here's how we can be sure that we know God in the right way: Keep his commandments.... The one who keeps God's word is the person in whom we see God's mature love. This is the only way to be sure we're in God. Anyone who claims to be intimate with God ought to live the same kind of life Jesus lived.

1 John 2:3,5-6

The Friend, the Holy Spirit whom the Father will send at my request, will make everything plain to you. He will remind you of all the things I have told you. I'm leaving you well and whole. That's my parting gift to you.

John 14:26-27

Appreciate your pastoral leaders who gave you the Word of God. Take a good look at the way they live, and let their faithfulness instruct you, as well as their truthfulness. There should be a consistency that runs through us all. For Jesus doesn't change—yesterday, today, tomorrow, he's always totally himself.

Hebrews 13:7-8

Don't fool yourself. Don't think that you can be wise merely by being up-to-date with the times. Be God's fool—that's the path to true wisdom. What the world calls smart, God calls stupid.

1 Corinthians 3:18-19

This Christian life is a great mystery, far exceeding our understanding, but some things are clear enough: He appeared in a human body, was proved right by the invisible Spirit, was seen by angels. He was proclaimed among all kinds of peoples, believed in all over the world, taken up into heavenly glory.

1 Timothy 3:16

Jesus, seeing that everything had been completed so that the Scripture record might also be complete, then said, "I'm thirsty...." After he took the wine, Jesus said, "It's done...complete." Bowing his head, he offered up his spirit.

John 19:28-30

Put GOD in charge of your work,
then what you've planned will take place....
We plan the way we want to live,
but only GOD makes us able to live it.

Proverbs 16:3,9

....

September 30

If you make Insight your priority,
and won't take no for an answer,
Searching for it like a prospector panning for gold,
like an adventurer on a treasure hunt,
Believe me, before you know it Fear-of-GOD will be yours;
you'll have come upon the Knowledge of God.

Proverbs 2:3-5

April 3

Grace and peace to you many times over as you deepen in your experience with God and Jesus, our Master. Everything that goes into a life of pleasing God has been miraculously given to us by getting to know, personally and intimately, the One who invited us to God. The best invitation we ever received!

2 Peter 1:2

September 29

After the Sabbath, as the first light of the new week dawned, Mary Magdalene and the other Mary came to keep vigil at the tomb. Suddenly the earth reeled and rocked under their feet as God's angel came down from heaven, came right up to where they were standing. He rolled back the stone and then sat on it. Shafts of lightning blazed from him. His garments shimmered snow-white.

Matthew 28:1-3

*You're all I want in heaven!
You're all I want on earth!...
I'm in the very presence of God—
oh, how refreshing it is!*

Psalm 73:25,28

September 28

Do you want to stand out? Then step down. Be a servant. If you puff yourself up, you'll get the wind knocked out of you. But if you're content to simply be yourself, your life will count for plenty.

Matthew 23:11-12

The whole point of what we're urging is simply *love*—
love uncontaminated by self-interest and
counterfeit faith, a life open to God.

1 Timothy 1:5

September 27

The angel spoke to the women: "There is nothing to fear here. I know you're looking for Jesus, the One they nailed to the cross. He is not here. He was raised, just as he said."

Matthew 28:5-6

We use our powerful God-tools for smashing warped philosophies, tearing down barriers erected against the truth of God, fitting every loose thought and emotion and impulse into the structure of life shaped by Christ. Our tools are ready at hand for clearing the ground of every obstruction and building lives of obedience into maturity.

2 Corinthians 10:5-6

September 26

This is the crisis we're in: God-light streamed into the world, but men and women everywhere ran for the darkness. They went for the darkness because they were not really interested in pleasing God.... But anyone working and living in truth and reality welcomes God-light so the work can be seen for the God-work it is.

John 3:19,21

God—you're my God! I can't get enough of you!
I've worked up such hunger and thirst for God,
   traveling across dry and weary deserts.
So here I am in the place of worship, eyes open,
   drinking in your strength and glory.
In your generous love I am really living at last!

Psalm 63:1-3

Jesus spoke to her, "Woman, why do you weep? Who are you looking for?"
She, thinking that he was the gardener, said, "Mister, if you took him, tell me where you put him so I can care for him." Jesus said, "Mary." Turning to face him, she said in Hebrew, "Rabboni!" meaning "Teacher!"

John 20:15-16

You're done with that old life. It's like a filthy set of ill-fitting clothes you've stripped off and put in the fire. Now you're dressed in a new wardrobe. Every item of your new way of life is custom-made by the Creator, with his label on it. All the old fashions are now obsolete.

Colossians 3:9-10

"The Marriage of the Lamb has come;
his Wife has made herself ready.
She was given a bridal gown
of bright and shining linen.
The linen is the righteousness of the saints."
The Angel said to me, "Write this: 'Blessed are those invited
to the Wedding Supper of the Lamb.'"

Revelation 19:7-9

The person who lives in right relationship with God does it by embracing what God arranges for him. Doing things for God is the opposite of entering into what God does for you.... "The person who believes God, is set right by God—and that's the real life."

Galatians 3:11

Later on that day, the disciples had gathered together, but, fearful of the Jews, had locked all the doors in the house. Jesus entered, stood among them, and said, "Peace to you." Then he showed them his hands and side. The disciples, seeing the Master with their own eyes, were exuberant. Jesus repeated his greeting: "Peace to you. Just as the Father sent me, I send you."

John 20:19-21

You're blessed when you're at the end of your rope.
With less of you there is more of God and his rule.
You're blessed when you feel you've lost what
is most dear to you. Only then can you be
embraced by the One most dear to you.

Matthew 5:3-4

So, chosen by God for this new life of love, dress in the wardrobe God picked out for you: compassion, kindness, humility, quiet strength, discipline.... Forgive as quickly and completely as the Master forgave you. And regardless of what else you put on, wear love. It's your basic, all-purpose garment. Never be without it.

Colossians 3:12-14

If those who get what God gives them only get it by doing everything they are told to do and filling out all the right forms properly signed, that eliminates personal trust completely and turns the promise into an ironclad contract!... But if there is no contract in the first place, simply a promise—and God's promise at that—you can't break it.

Romans 4:14-15

At one time you all had your backs turned to God.... But now, by giving himself completely at the Cross, actually *dying* for you, Christ brought you over to God's side and put your lives together, whole and holy in his presence. You don't walk away from a gift like that! You stay grounded and steady in that bond of trust.... There is no other Message—just this one.

Colossians 1:21-23

The deeper your love, the higher it goes;
every cloud is a flag to your faithfulness.
Soar high in the skies, O God!
Cover the whole earth with your glory!

Psalm 57:10-11

September 20

*L*ove...isn't always "me first,"
Doesn't fly off the handle,
Doesn't keep score of the sins of others,
Doesn't revel when others grovel,
Takes pleasure in the flowering of truth.

1 Corinthians 13:4-6

April 13

[God] thought of everything, provided for everything we could possibly need, letting us in on the plans he took such delight in making. He set it all out before us in Christ, a long-range plan in which everything would be brought together and summed up in him, everything in deepest heaven, everything on planet earth.

Ephesians 1:8-10

September 19

*H*e lived a selfless, obedient life and then died a selfless, obedient death—and the worst kind of death at that: a crucifixion. Because of that obedience, God lifted him high and honored him far beyond anyone or anything, ever, so that all created beings in heaven and on earth...will bow in worship before this Jesus Christ, and call out in praise that he is the Master of all, to the glorious honor of God the Father.

Philippians 2:8-11

April 14

You know me inside and out, you hold me together,
you never fail to stand me tall in your presence
so I can look you in the eye.

Psalm 41:12

September 18

They hit me when I was down,
but GOD stuck by me.
He stood me up on a wide-open field;
I stood there saved—surprised to be loved!

Psalm 18:18-19

You let [your] distress bring you to God, not drive you from him. The result was all gain, no loss. Distress that drives us to God does that. It turns us around. It gets us back in the way of salvation. We never regret that kind of pain. But those who let distress drive them away from God are full of regrets.

2 Corinthians 7:9-10

You don't have to wait for the End. I am, right now, Resurrection and Life. The one who believes in me, even though he or she dies, will live. And everyone who lives believing in me does not ultimately die at all.

John 11:25-26

Real religion, the kind that passes muster before God the Father, is this: Reach out to the homeless and loveless in their plight, and guard against corruption from the godless world.

James 1:27

September 16

So where can you find someone truly wise, truly educated, truly intelligent in this day and age?... Since the world in all its fancy wisdom never had a clue when it came to knowing God, God in his wisdom took delight in using what the world considered dumb...to bring those who trust him into the way of salvation.... We go right on proclaiming Christ, the Crucified.

1 Corinthians 1:20-22

God means what he says. What he says goes. His powerful Word is sharp as a surgeon's scalpel, cutting through everything, whether doubt or defense, laying us open to listen and obey. Nothing and no one is impervious to God's Word. We can't get away from it—no matter what.

Hebrews 4:12

September 15

Christ...presented himself for this sacrificial death when we were far too weak and rebellious to do anything to get ourselves ready.... We can understand someone dying for a person worth dying for, and we can understand how someone good and noble could inspire us to selfless sacrifice. But God put his love on the line for us by offering his Son in sacrificial death while we were of no use whatever to him.

Romans 5:6-8

Saving is all his idea, and all his work. All we do is trust him enough to let him do it. It's God's gift from start to finish! We don't play the major role. If we did, we'd probably go around bragging that we'd done the whole thing!

Ephesians 2:8-9

September 14

Examine me, GOD...
Make sure I'm fit inside and out
So I never lose sight of your love,
But keep in step with you,
never missing a beat.

Psalm 26:2-3

The law code...finally adds up to this: Love other people as well as you do yourself. You can't go wrong when you love others. When you add up everything in the law code, the sum total is *love*.

Romans 13:9-10

We continue to shout our praise even when we're hemmed in with troubles, because we know how troubles can develop passionate patience in us, and how that patience in turn forges the tempered steel of virtue, keeping us alert for whatever God will do next. In alert expectancy such as this…we can't round up enough containers to hold everything God generously pours into our lives through the Holy Spirit!

Romans 5:3-5

*I'm leaping and singing in the circle of your love...
Blessed GOD!
His love is the wonder of the world.*

Psalm 31:7,21

September 12

And me? I plan on looking
you full in the face. When I get up,
I'll see your full stature
and live heaven on earth.

Psalm 17:15

April 21

God's Spirit touches our spirits and confirms who we really are. We know who he is, and we know who we are: Father and children. And we know we are going to get what's coming to us—an unbelievable inheritance! We go through exactly what Christ goes through. If we go through the hard times with him, then we're certainly going to go through the good times with him!

Romans 8:16-17

September 11

This is how we've come to understand and experience love: Christ sacrificed his life for us. This is why we ought to live sacrificially for our fellow believers, and not just be out for ourselves. If you see some brother or sister in need and have the means to do something about it but turn a cold shoulder and do nothing, what happens to God's love? It disappears. And you made it disappear.

1 John 3:16-17

April 22

Pursue a righteous life—a life of wonder, faith, love, steadiness, courtesy. Run hard and fast in the faith. Seize the eternal life, the life you were called to, the life you so fervently embraced.

1 Timothy 6:11-12

Septmeber 10

God can pour on the blessings in astonishing ways so that you're ready for anything and everything, more than just ready to do what needs to be done.... This most generous God who gives seed to the farmer that becomes bread for your meals is more than extravagant with you...so that you can be generous in every way, producing with us great praise to God.

2 Corinthians 9:8

Immense in mercy and with an incredible love, [God] embraced us. He took our sin-dead lives and made us alive in Christ. He did all this on his own, with no help from us! Then he picked us up and set us down in highest heaven in company with Jesus, our Messiah. Now God has us where he wants us, with all the time in this world and the next to shower grace and kindness upon us in Christ Jesus.

Ephesians 2:4-7

If you wake me each morning with the
sound of your loving voice,
I'll go to sleep each night trusting in you.
Point out the road I must travel;
I'm all ears, all eyes before you.

Psalm 143:8

*G*OD made my life complete
when I placed all the pieces before him.
When I got my act together,
he gave me a fresh start....
GOD rewrote the text of my life
when I opened the book of my heart to his eyes.

Psalm 18:20,24

September 8

And who would dare tangle with God by messing with one of God's chosen? Who would dare even to point a finger? The One who died for us—who was raised to life for us!—is in the presence of God at this very moment sticking up for us. Do you think anyone is going to be able to drive a wedge between us and Christ's love for us? There is no way!

Romans 8:33-35

By entering through faith into what God has always wanted to do for us—set us right with him, make us fit for him—we have it all together with God.... We throw open our doors to God and discover at the same moment that he has already thrown open his door to us. We find ourselves standing where we always hoped we might stand—out in the wide open spaces of God's grace and glory, standing tall and shouting our praise.

Romans 5:1-2

If you decide for God, living a life of God-worship, it follows that...there is far more to your life than the food you put in your stomach, more to your outer appearance than the clothes you hang on your body. Look at the birds, free and unfettered, not tied down to a job description, careless in the care of God. And you count far more to him than birds.

Matthew 6:25-26

Let's practice real love. This is the only way we'll know we're living truly, living in God's reality. It's also the way to shut down debilitating self-criticism.... For God is greater than our worried hearts and knows more about us than we do ourselves. And friends, once that's taken care of and we're no longer accusing or condemning ourselves, we're bold and free before God!

1 John 3:18-21

$\mathcal{G}$OD is all mercy and grace—
not quick to anger, is rich in love.
GOD is good to one and all;
everything he does is suffused with grace....
GOD always does what he says,
and is gracious in everything he does.

Psalm 145:8-9,13

....

*L*ive creatively, friends. If someone falls into sin, forgivingly restore him, saving your critical comments for yourself. You might be needing forgiveness before the day's out. Stoop down and reach out to those who are oppressed. Share their burdens, and so complete Christ's law.

Galatians 6:1-2

Jesus is "the stone you masons threw out, which is now the cornerstone." Salvation comes no other way; no other name has been or will be given to us by which we can be saved, only this one.

Acts 4:11-12

April 28

Keep your eyes on *Jesus*, who both began and finished this race we're in. Study how he did it. Because he never lost sight of where he was headed—that exhilarating finish in and with God—he could put up with anything along the way: cross, shame, whatever. And now he's *there*, in the place of honor, right alongside God.

Hebrews 12:2

September 4

He used his servant body to carry our sins to the Cross so we could be rid of sin, free to live the right way. His wounds became your healing. You were lost sheep with no idea who you were or where you were going. Now you're named and kept for good by the Shepherd of your souls.

1 Peter 2:24-25

I love you, GOD—you make me strong.
GOD is bedrock under my feet,
the castle in which I live, my rescuing knight.
My God—the high crag where I run for dear life.

Psalm 18:1-2

September 3

God thunders across the waters,
Brilliant, his voice and his face, streaming brightness—
God, across the flood waters.
God's thunder tympanic,
God's thunder symphonic.

Psalm 29:3-4

𝒥'm absolutely convinced that nothing—nothing living or dead, angelic or demonic, today or tomorrow, high or low, thinkable or unthinkable—absolutely nothing can get between us and God's love because of the way that Jesus our Master has embraced us.

Romans 8:38-39

*L*ove mixed with faith be yours from God the Father and from the Master, Jesus Christ. Pure grace and nothing but grace be with all who love our Master, Jesus Christ.

Ephesians 6:23-24

In the Messiah, in Christ, God leads us from place to place in one perpetual victory parade. Through us, he brings knowledge of Christ. Everywhere we go, people breathe in the exquisite fragrance. Because of Christ, we give off a sweet scent rising to God, which is recognized by those on the way of salvation—an aroma redolent with life.

2 Corinthians 2:14-15

September 1

So here's what I want you to do, God helping you: Take your everyday, ordinary life—your sleeping, eating, going-to-work, and walking-around life—and place it before God as an offering. Embracing what God does for you is the best thing you can do for him.

Romans 12:1

....

I call to you, God, because I'm sure of an answer....
Keep your eye on me;
hide me under your cool wing feathers.

Psalm 17:6,8

The person who trusts me will not only do what I'm doing but even greater things, because I, on my way to the Father, am giving you the same work to do that I've been doing. From now on, whatever you request along the lines of who I am and what I am doing, I'll do it. That's how the Father will be seen for who he is in the Son. I mean it. Whatever you request in this way, I'll do.

John 14:12-14

I ask—ask the God of our Master, Jesus Christ, the God of glory—to make you intelligent and discerning in knowing him personally, your eyes focused and clear, so that you can see exactly what it is he is calling you to do, grasp the immensity of this glorious way of life he has for Christians, oh, the utter extravagance of his work in us who trust him—endless energy, boundless strength!

Ephesians 1:17-19

You get us ready for life:
you probe for our soft spots,
you knock off our rough edges.
And I'm feeling so fit, so safe:
made right, kept right.
God in solemn honor does things right.

Psalm 7:9-11

At the time, discipline isn't much fun. It always feels like it's going against the grain. Later, of course, it pays off handsomely, for it's the well-trained who find themselves mature in their relationship with God.

Hebrews 12:11

If I speak with human eloquence and angelic ecstasy but don't love, I'm nothing but the creaking of a rusty gate. If I speak God's Word with power, revealing all his mysteries and making everything plain as day, and if I have faith that says to a mountain, "Jump," and it jumps, but I don't love, I'm nothing.

1 Corinthians 13:1-2

I look up at your macro-skies, dark and enormous,
your handmade sky-jewelry,
Moon and stars mounted in their settings.
Then I look at my micro-self and wonder,
Why do you bother with us?
Why take a second look our way?

Psalm 8:3-4

It is absolutely clear that God has called you to a free life. Just make sure that you don't use this freedom as an excuse to do whatever you want to do and destroy your freedom. Rather, use your freedom to serve one another in love; that's how freedom grows. For everything we know about God's Word is summed up in a single sentence: Love others as you love yourself. That's an act of true freedom.

Galatians 5:13-14

May 6

God...entered the disordered mess of struggling humanity in order to set it right once and for all. The law code, weakened as it always was by fractured human nature, could never have done that.... And now what the law code asked for but we couldn't deliver is accomplished as we, instead of redoubling our own efforts, simply embrace what the Spirit is doing in us.

Romans 8:3-4

You've been a safe place for me,
a good place to hide.
Strong God, I'm watching you do it,
I can always count on you—
God, my dependable love.

Psalm 59:16-17

Did you receive the Holy Spirit when you believed?
Did you take God into your mind only, or did you also
embrace him with your heart? Did he get inside you?

Acts 19:2

August 26

God is love. When we take up permanent residence in
a life of love, we live in God and God lives in us. This
way, love has the run of the house, becomes at home
and mature in us, so that we're free of worry on
Judgment Day—our standing in the world
is identical with Christ's.

1 John 4:16-17

Why is everyone hungry for *more*?...
I have God's more-than-enough,
More joy in one ordinary day....
At day's end I'm ready for sound sleep,
For you, GOD, have put my life back together.

Psalm 4:6-8

August 25

*L*ove your enemies. Let them bring out the best in you, not the worst. When someone gives you a hard time, respond with the energies of prayer, for then you are working out of your true selves, your God-created selves. This is what God does. He gives his best—the sun to warm and the rain to nourish—to everyone.

Matthew 5:44-45

*Because of the Master,
we have great confidence in you....
May the Master take you by the hand
and lead you along the path of God's
love and Christ's endurance.*

2 Thessalonians 3:4-5

August 24

What a wildly wonderful world, GOD!
You made it all, with Wisdom at your side,
made earth overflow with your wonderful creations....
All the creatures look expectantly to you....
The glory of GOD—let it last forever!
Let GOD enjoy his creation!

Psalm 104:24,27,31

I'm not saying that I have this all together, that I have it made. But I am well on my way, reaching out for Christ, who has so wondrously reached out for me. Friends, don't get me wrong: By no means do I count myself an expert in all of this, but I've got my eye on the goal, where God is beckoning us onward—to Jesus. I'm off and running, and I'm not turning back.

Philippians 3:12-14

Sin didn't, and doesn't, have a chance in competition with the aggressive forgiveness we call grace. When it's sin versus grace, grace wins hands down. All sin can do is threaten us with death, and that's the end of it. Grace, because God is putting everything together again through the Messiah, invites us into life—a life that goes on and on and on, world without end.

Romans 5:20-21

I saw a Great White Throne and the One Enthroned. Nothing could stand before or against the Presence, nothing in Heaven, nothing on earth. And then I saw all the dead, great and small, standing there—before the Throne! And books were opened. Then another book was opened: the Book of Life. The dead were judged by what was written in the books, by the way they had lived.

Revelation 20:11-12

Your eye is a lamp, lighting up your whole body. If you live wide-eyed in wonder and belief, your body fills up with light.... Keep your eyes open, your lamp burning, so you don't get musty and murky. Keep your life as well-lighted as your best-lighted room.

Luke 11:34-36

I look behind me and you're there,
then up ahead and you're there, too—
your reassuring presence, coming and going.
This is too much, too wonderful—
I can't take it all in!

Psalm 139:5-6

If God gives such attention to the appearance of wildflowers—most of which are never even seen—don't you think he'll attend to you, take pride in you, do his best for you? What I'm trying to do here is to get you to relax, to not be so preoccupied with getting, so you can respond to God's giving.

Matthew 6:30-31

There is no room in love for fear. Well-formed love banishes fear. Since fear is crippling, a fearful life—fear of death, fear of judgment—is one not yet fully formed in love.

1 John 4:18

For my part, I am going to boast about nothing but the Cross of our Master, Jesus Christ. Because of that Cross, I have been crucified in relation to the world, set free from the stifling atmosphere of pleasing others and fitting into the little patterns that they dictate. Can't you see the central issue in all this? It is not what you and I do.... It is what God is doing, and he is creating something totally new, a free life!

Galatians 6:14-15

While he lived on earth, anticipating death, Jesus cried out in pain and wept in sorrow as he offered up priestly prayers to God. Because he honored God, God answered him. Though he was God's Son, he learned trusting-obedience by what he suffered, just as we do.

Hebrews 5:7-8

August 19

*G*OD's works are so great, worth
A lifetime of study—endless enjoyment!
Splendor and beauty mark his craft;
His generosity never gives out.
His miracles are his memorial—
This GOD of Grace, this GOD of Love.

Psalm 111:2-4

And that's about it, friends. Be cheerful. Keep things in good repair. Keep your spirits up. Think in harmony. Be agreeable. Do all that, and the God of love and peace will be with you.... The amazing grace of the Master, Jesus Christ, the extravagant love of God, the intimate friendship of the Holy Spirit, be with all of you.

2 Corinthians 13:11,14

When they were together for the last time they asked, "Master, are you going to restore the kingdom to Israel now? Is this the time?" He told them, "You don't get to know the time. Timing is the Father's business. What you'll get is the Holy Spirit. And when the Holy Spirit comes on you, you will be able to be my witnesses in Jerusalem, all over Judea and Samaria, even to the ends of the world."

Acts 1:6-8

May 16

You know well enough from your own experience that there are some acts of so-called freedom that destroy freedom. Offer yourselves to sin, for instance, and it's your last free act. But offer yourselves to the ways of God and the freedom never quits. All your lives you've let sin tell you what to do. But thank God you've started listening to a new master, one whose commands set you free to live openly in his freedom!

Romans 6:16

Christ...was sheer weakness and humiliation when he was killed on the Cross, but oh, he's alive now—in the mighty power of God!

2 Corinthians 13:3-4

May 17

The people I love, I call to account—prod
and correct and guide so that they'll live at their best.
Up on your feet, then! About face! Run after God!

Revelation 3:19

August 16

God's love is meteoric,
his loyalty astronomic,
His purpose titanic,
his verdicts oceanic.
Yet in his largeness
nothing gets lost.

Psalm 36:5-6

May 18

Now to him who can keep you on your feet, standing tall in his bright presence, fresh and celebrating—to our one God, our only Savior, through Jesus Christ, our Master, be glory, majesty, strength, and rule before all time, and now, and to the end of all time.

Jude 1:24-25

Because of the sacrifice of the Messiah, his blood poured out on the altar of the Cross, we're a free people—free of penalties and punishments chalked up by all our misdeeds. And not just barely free, either. Abundantly free!

Ephesians 1:7

*H*allelujah! You who serve God, praise God!
Just to speak his name is praise!
Just to remember God is a blessing—
now and tomorrow and always.
From east to west, from dawn to dusk,
keep lifting all your praises to God!

Psalm 113:1-3

Are you tired? Worn out? Burned out on religion? Come to me. Get away with me and you'll recover your life. I'll show you how to take a real rest. Walk with me and work with me—watch how I do it. Learn the unforced rhythms of grace. I won't lay anything heavy or ill-fitting on you. Keep company with me and you'll learn to live freely and lightly.

Matthew 11:28-30

God is a living, personal presence.... And when God is personally present, a living Spirit, that old, constricting legislation is recognized as obsolete.... Nothing between us and God, our faces shining with the brightness of his face. And so we are transfigured much like the Messiah, our lives gradually becoming brighter and more beautiful as God enters our lives and we become like him.

2 Corinthians 3:17-18

Have you ever come on anything quite like this extravagant generosity of God, this deep, deep wisdom? It's way over our heads. We'll never figure it out. "Is there anyone around who can explain God? Anyone smart enough to tell him what to do?..." Everything comes from him; Everything happens through him; Everything ends up in him. Always glory! Always praise!

Romans 11:33-36

....

Wives, understand and support your husbands in ways that show your support for Christ. The husband provides leadership to his wife the way Christ does to his church, not by domineering but by cherishing. So just as the church submits to Christ as he exercises such leadership, wives should likewise submit to their husbands.

Ephesians 5:22-24

*God's glory is on tour in the skies...
unspoken truth is spoken everywhere.*

Psalm 19:1,4

May 22

What marvelous love the Father has extended to us! Just look at it—we're called children of God! That's who we really are.... And that's only the beginning. Who knows how we'll end up! What we know is that when Christ is openly revealed, we'll see him—and in seeing him, become like him. All of us who look forward to his Coming stay ready, with the glistening purity of Jesus' life as a model for our own.

1 John 3:1-3

August 11

I can't tell you how much I long for you to enter this wide-open, spacious life.... Your lives aren't small, but you're living them in a small way. I'm speaking as plainly as I can and with great affection. Open up your lives. Live openly and expansively!

2 Corinthians 6:11-13

God, my shepherd! I don't need a thing. You have bedded me down in lush meadows, you find me quiet pools to drink from. True to your word, you let me catch my breath and send me in the right direction. Even when the way goes through Death Valley, I'm not afraid when you walk at my side.

Psalm 23:1-4

August 10

This is your Father you are dealing with, and he knows better than you what you need. With a God like this loving you, you can pray very simply. Like this: "Our Father in heaven, reveal who you are. Set the world right; do what's best—as above, so below."

Matthew 6:8-10

My sheep recognize my voice. I know them, and they follow me. I give them real and eternal life. They are protected from the Destroyer for good. No one can steal them from out of my hand. The Father who put them under my care is so much greater than the Destroyer and Thief. No one could ever get them away from him.
I and the Father are one heart and mind.

John 10:27-30

I'll run the course you lay out for me
if you'll just show me how.
GOD, teach me lessons for living
so I can stay the course.
Give me insight so I can do what you tell me—
my whole life one long, obedient response.

Psalm 119:32-34

I [Wisdom] love those who love me;
those who look for me find me.
Wealth and Glory accompany me—
also substantial Honor and a Good Name.
My benefits are worth more than a big salary,
even a *very* big salary;
the returns on me exceed any imaginable bonus.

Proverbs 8:17-19

What matters is not your outer appearance—the styling of your hair, the jewelry you wear, the cut of your clothes—but your inner disposition. Cultivate inner beauty, the gentle, gracious kind that God delights in.

1 Peter 3:3-4

God is light, pure light; there's not a trace of darkness in him. If we claim that we experience a shared life with him and continue to stumble around in the dark, we're obviously lying.... But if we walk in the light, God himself being the light, we also experience a shared life with one another, as the sacrificed blood of Jesus, God's Son, purges all our sin.

1 John 1.5-7

God can do anything, you know—far more than
you could ever imagine or guess or request
in your wildest dreams!...
Glory to God in the church!
Glory to God in the Messiah, in Jesus!
Glory down all the generations!
Glory through all millennia!

Ephesians 3:20-21

May 27

Glory and strength to Christ, who loves us,
who blood-washed our sins from our lives,
Who made us a Kingdom, Priests for his Father,
forever—and yes, he's on his way!
Riding the clouds, he'll be seen by every eye.

Revelation 1:5-7

God, you did everything you promised,
and I'm thanking you with all my heart.
You pulled me from the brink of death,
my feet from the cliff-edge of doom.
Now I stroll at leisure with God
in the sunlit fields of life.

Psalm 56:12-13

With God, one day is as good as a thousand years, a thousand years as a day. God isn't late with his promise as some measure lateness. He is restraining himself on account of you, holding back the End because he doesn't want anyone lost. He's giving everyone space and time to change.

2 Peter 3:8-9

Don't become so well-adjusted to your culture that you fit into it without even thinking. Instead, fix your attention on God. You'll be changed from the inside out. Readily recognize what he wants from you, and quickly respond to it. Unlike the culture around you, always dragging you down to its level of immaturity, God brings the best out of you, develops well-formed maturity in you.

Romans 12:2

You know me inside and out…
You know exactly how I was made, bit by bit,
how I was sculpted from nothing into something.
Like an open book, you watched me grow
from conception to birth;
all the stages of my life were spread out before you…
before I'd even lived one day.
Psalm 139:15-16

Go after a life of love as if your life depended on it—
because it does. Give yourselves to the gifts God gives
you. Most of all, try to proclaim his truth.

1 Corinthians 14:1

Let me tell you something wonderful, a mystery I'll probably never fully understand. We're not all going to die—but we are all going to be changed.... On signal from that trumpet from heaven, the dead will be up and out of their graves, beyond the reach of death, never to die again. At the same moment and in the same way, we'll all be changed.

1 Corinthians 15:51-52

𝒢OD promises to love me all day,
sing songs all through the night!
My life is God's prayer.

Psalm 42:8

....

Keep a firm grip on the faith. The suffering won't last forever. It won't be long before this generous God who has great plans for us in Christ—eternal and glorious plans they are!—will have you put together and on your feet for good. He gets the last word; yes, he does.

1 Peter 5:9-11

There has never been the slightest doubt in my mind
that the God who started this great work in you would
keep at it and bring it to a flourishing finish on
the very day Christ Jesus appears.

Philippians 1:6

"As I live and breathe," God says,
"every knee will bow before me;
Every tongue will tell the honest truth
that I and only I am God."

Romans 14:11

August 1

If you're a hard worker and do a good job, you deserve your pay; we don't call your wages a gift. But if you see that the job is too big for you, that it's something only *God* can do, and you trust him to do it—you could never do it for yourself no matter how hard and long you worked—well, that trusting-him-to-do-it is what gets you set right with God, *by* God. Sheer gift.

Romans 4:4-5

ℬe prepared. You're up against far more than you can handle on your own. Take all the help you can get, every weapon God has issued, so that when it's all over but the shouting you'll still be on your feet.

Ephesians 6:13

Outlast the sun, outlive the moon—
age after age after age.
Be rainfall on cut grass,
earth-refreshing rain showers.
Let righteousness burst into blossom
and peace abound until the moon fades to nothing.
Rule from sea to sea, from the River to the Rim.

Psalm 72:5-8

*Yes, because GOD's your refuge,
the High God your very own home,
Evil can't get close to you,
harm can't get through the door.
He ordered his angels
to guard you wherever you go.*

Psalm 91:9-11

You're blessed when you care. At the moment of being "care-full," you find yourselves cared for. You're blessed when you get your inside world—your mind and heart— put right. Then you can see God in the outside world.

Matthew 5:7-8

In the original creation, God made male and female to be together. Because of this, a man leaves father and mother, and in marriage he becomes one flesh with a woman—no longer two individuals, but forming a new unity. Because God created this organic union of the two sexes, no one should desecrate his art by cutting them apart.

Mark 10:6-9

July 29

We look at this Son and see the God who cannot be seen. We look at this Son and see God's original purpose in everything created. For everything, absolutely everything, above and below, visible and invisible, rank after rank after rank of angels—*everything* got started in him and finds its purpose in him.

Colossians 1:15-16

*L*ove never gives up.
Love cares more for others than for self.
Love doesn't want what it doesn't have.
Love doesn't strut,
Doesn't have a swelled head,
Doesn't force itself on others.

1 Corinthians 13:4-5

July 28

I'm an open book to you;
even from a distance, you know what I'm thinking.
You know when I leave and when I get back;
I'm never out of your sight.
You know everything I'm going to say
before I start the first sentence.

Psalm 139:2-4

June 6

Not one is missing, not one forgotten. God the Father has his eye on each of you, and has determined by the work of the Spirit to keep you obedient through the sacrifice of Jesus. May everything good from God be yours!

1 Peter 1:1-2

I am the Gate for the sheep.... Anyone who goes through me will be cared for—will freely go in and out, and find pasture. A thief is only there to steal and kill and destroy. I came so they can have real and eternal life, more and better life than they ever dreamed of.

John 10:7-10

What a stack of blessing you have piled up
for those who worship you,
Ready and waiting for all who run to you
to escape an unkind world.
You hide them safely away
from the opposition.

Psalm 31:19-20

I've learned by now to be quite content whatever my circumstances. I'm just as happy with little as with much, with much as with little. I've found the recipe for being happy whether full or hungry, hands full or hands empty. Whatever I have, wherever I am, I can make it through anything in the One who makes me who I am.

Philippians 4:11-13

Make this your common practice: Confess your sins to each other and pray for each other so that you can live together whole and healed. The prayer of a person living right with God is something powerful to be reckoned with.

James 5:16

Don't grieve God. Don't break his heart. His Holy Spirit, moving and breathing in you, is the most intimate part of your life, making you fit for himself. Don't take such a gift for granted.

Ephesians 4:30

*You're blessed when you've lost it all.
God's kingdom is there for the finding....
You're blessed when the tears flow freely.
Joy comes with the morning.*

Luke 6:20-21

July 24

*You're blessed when you stay on course,
walking steadily on the road revealed by GOD.
You're blessed when you follow his directions,
doing your best to find him.*

Psalm 119:1-2

In simple humility, let our gardener, God, landscape you with the Word, making a salvation-garden of your life.

James 1:21

July 23

I want you woven into a tapestry of love, in touch with everything there is to know of God. Then you will have minds confident and at rest, focused on Christ, God's great mystery. All the richest treasures of wisdom and knowledge are embedded in that mystery and nowhere else.

Colossians 2:2-3

June 11

Blessed are the people who know the passwords of praise.... Delighted, they dance all day long; they know who you are, what you do—they can't keep it quiet! Your vibrant beauty has gotten inside us—you've been so good to us! We're walking on air! All we are and have we owe to GOD!

Psalm 89:15-18

July 22

No test or temptation that comes your way is beyond the course of what others have had to face. All you need to remember is that God will never let you down; he'll never let you be pushed past your limit; he'll always be there to help you come through it.

1 Corinthians 10:13

June 12

"*L*ove others as you love yourself...."
Kind mercy wins over harsh
judgment every time.

James 2:8,13

....

July 21

Basically, all of us...start out in identical conditions, which is to say that we all start out as sinners. Scripture leaves no doubt about it: "There's nobody living right, not even one, nobody who knows the score, nobody alert for God. They've all taken the wrong turn; they've all wandered down blind alleys. No one's living right; I can't find a single one."

Romans 3:9-12

*O*h! May the God of green hope fill you up with joy,
fill you up with peace, so that your believing lives,
filled with the life-giving energy of the Holy Spirit,
will brim over with hope!

Romans 15:13

Remember: A stingy planter gets a stingy crop; a lavish planter gets a lavish crop. I want each of you to take plenty of time to think it over, and make up your own mind what you will give.... God loves it when the giver delights in the giving.

2 Corinthians 9:6-7

....

*The moment I called out, you stepped in;
you made my life large with strength....
Finish what you started in me, G*OD.
Your love is eternal.

Psalm 138:3,8

July 19

Now GOD, don't hold out on me,
don't hold back your passion.
Your love and truth
are all that keeps me together.

Psalm 40:11

June 15

Consider it a sheer gift, friends, when tests and challenges come at you from all sides. You know that under pressure, your faith-life is forced into the open and shows its true colors. So don't try to get out of anything prematurely. Let it do its work so you become mature and well-developed, not deficient in any way.

James 1:2-4

July 18

We preach Christ, warning people not to add to the Message. We teach in a spirit of profound common sense so that we can bring each person to maturity.
To be mature is to be basic.
Christ! No more, no less.

Colossians 1:28

Whoever wants to be great must become a servant. Whoever wants to be first among you must be your slave. That is what the Son of Man has done: He came to serve, not be served—and then to give away his life in exchange for the many who are held hostage.

Matthew 20:26-28

May God himself, the God who makes everything holy and whole, make you holy and whole, put you together—spirit, soul, and body—and keep you fit for the coming of our Master, Jesus Christ. The One who called you is completely dependable. If he said it, he'll do it!

1 Thessalonians 5:23-24

*E*verything in the world is about to be wrapped up,
so take nothing for granted. Stay wide-awake in prayer.
Most of all, love each other as if your life depended on it.
Love makes up for practically anything.

1 Peter 4:7-8

I will put together my church, a church so expansive with energy that not even the gates of hell will be able to keep it out. And that's not all. You will have complete and free access to God's kingdom, keys to open any and every door: no more barriers between heaven and earth, earth and heaven. A yes on earth is yes in heaven.
A no on earth is no in heaven.

Matthew 16:18-19

June 18

His huge outstretched arms protect you—
under them you're perfectly safe;
his arms fend off all harm....
No harm will even graze you.
You'll stand untouched, watch it all from a distance.

Psalm 91:4,8

God, the one and only—
I'll wait as long as he says.
Everything I need comes from him....
He's solid rock under my feet,
breathing room for my soul.

Psalm 62:1-2

June 19

Stay on good terms with each other, held together by love. Be ready with a meal or a bed when it's needed. Why, some have extended hospitality to angels without ever knowing it! Regard prisoners as if you were in prison with them. Look on victims of abuse as if what happened to them had happened to you.

Hebrews 13:1-3

It's impossible to please God apart from faith. And why? Because anyone who wants to approach God must believe both that he exists *and* that he cares enough to respond to those who seek him.

Hebrews 11:6

If one man's sin put crowds of people at the dead-end abyss of separation from God, just think what God's gift poured through one man, Jesus Christ, will do!... If death got the upper hand through one man's wrongdoing, can you imagine the breathtaking recovery life makes...in those who grasp with both hands this wildly extravagant life-gift...that the one man Jesus Christ provides?

Romans 5:15,17

God plays no favorites! It makes no difference who you are or where you're from—if you want God and are ready to do as he says, the door is open. The Message he sent to the children of Israel—that through Jesus Christ everything is being put together again—well, he's doing it everywhere, among everyone.

Acts 10:34-36

June 21

Creation and creatures applaud you, GOD; your holy people bless you. They talk about the glories of your rule, they exclaim over your splendor, letting the world know of your power for good, the lavish splendor of your kingdom. Your kingdom is a kingdom eternal.

Psalm 145:10-13

*Affirm your promises to me—
promises made to all who fear you....
Let your love, GOD, shape my life
with salvation, exactly as you promised.*

Psalm 119:38,41

Make sure you don't take things for granted and go slack in working for the common good; share what you have with others. God takes particular pleasure in acts of worship—a different kind of "sacrifice"—that take place in kitchen and workplace and on the streets.

Hebrews 13:16

The first thing I want you to do is pray. Pray every way you know how, for everyone you know. Pray especially for rulers and their governments to rule well so we can be quietly about our business of living simply, in humble contemplation. This is the way our Savior God wants us to live.

1 Timothy 2:1-3

*W*hat a God! His road
stretches straight and smooth.
Every GOD-direction is road-tested.
Everyone who runs toward him makes it.
Is there any god like GOD?

Psalm 18:30-31

July 10

Don't assume that you know it all.
Run to GOD! Run from evil!
Your body will glow with health,
your very bones will vibrate with life!

Proverbs 3:7-8

Everyone has to die once, then face the consequences. Christ's death was also a one-time event, but it was a sacrifice that took care of sins forever. And so, when he next appears, the outcome for those eager to greet him is, precisely, *salvation*.

Hebrews 9:27-28

God...decided from the outset to shape the lives of those who love him along the same lines as the life of his Son.... He followed it up by calling people by name. After he called them by name, he set them on a solid basis with himself. And then, after getting them established, he stayed with them to the end, gloriously completing what he had begun.

Romans 8:29-30

June 25

And when you come before God...here's what I want you to do: Find a quiet, secluded place so you won't be tempted to role-play before God. Just be there as simply and honestly as you can manage. The focus will shift from you to God, and you will begin to sense his grace.

Matthew 6:5-6

𝒴ou'll do best by filling your minds and meditating on things true, noble, reputable, authentic, compelling, gracious—the best, not the worst; the beautiful, not the ugly; things to praise, not things to curse.... Do that, and God, who makes everything work together, will work you into his most excellent harmonies.

Philippians 4:8-9

*W*hat you say goes, GOD,
and *stays*, as permanent as the heavens.
Your truth never goes out of fashion;
it's as up-to-date as the earth when the sun comes up.
Your Word and truth are dependable as ever;
that's what you ordered—you set the earth going.

Psalm 119:89-91

And how blessed all those in whom you live,
whose lives become roads you travel;
They wind through lonesome valleys, come upon brooks,
discover cool springs and pools brimming with rain!
God-traveled, these roads curve up the mountain, and
at the last turn—Zion! God in full view!

Psalm 84:5-7

There's far more to life for us. We're citizens of high heaven! We're waiting the arrival of the Savior, the Master, Jesus Christ, who will transform our earthy bodies into glorious bodies like his own. He'll make us beautiful and whole with the same powerful skill by which he is putting everything as it should be, under and around him.

Philippians 3:20-21

This is a sure thing:
If we die with him, we'll live with him;
If we stick it out with him, we'll rule with him;
If we turn our backs on him, he'll turn his back on us;
If we give up on him, he does not give up—
for there's no way he can be false to himself.

2 Timothy 2:11-13

June 28

Jesus said, "Everyone who drinks this water will get thirsty again and again. Anyone who drinks the water I give will never thirst—not ever. The water I give will be an artesian spring within, gushing fountains of endless life."

John 4:13-14

What we...see is Jesus, made "not quite as high as angels," and then, through the experience of death, crowned so much higher than any angel, with a glory "bright with Eden's dawn light." In that death, by God's grace, he fully experienced death in every person's place. It makes good sense that the God who got everything started and keeps everything going now completes the work.

Hebrews 2:9-10

ℬe a good citizen. All governments are under God. Insofar as there is peace and order, it's God's order. So live responsibly as a citizen. If you're irresponsible to the state, then you're irresponsible with God, and God will hold you responsible.

Romans 13:1-2

July 4

Everyone's going through a refining fire sooner or later, but you'll be well-preserved, protected from the *eternal flames*. Be preservatives yourselves. Preserve the peace.

Mark 9:49-50

June 30

God wants the combination of his steady, constant calling and warm, personal counsel in Scripture to come to characterize us, keeping us alert for whatever he will do next.... Then we'll be a choir—not our voices only, but our very lives singing in harmony in a stunning anthem to the God and Father of our Master Jesus!

Romans 15:4,6

Oh my soul, bless GOD, don't forget a single blessing! He forgives your sins—every one. He heals your diseases—every one. He redeems you from hell—saves your life! He crowns you with love and mercy—a paradise crown. He wraps you in goodness—beauty eternal. He renews your youth—you're always young in his presence.

Psalm 103:2-5

July 1

God is strong, and he wants you strong. So take everything the Master has set out for you, well-made weapons of the best materials. And put them to use so you will be able to stand up to everything the Devil throws your way.

Ephesians 6:10-11

July 2